After Life...
Afterlife?

Other books by John Symons

All published by Shepheard-Walwyn

Love is His Meaning

"This book describes the tragedies that struck at the heart of a poor but devoted family. Humanity and the valour of the human spirit shine from every page" (This England).

It presents in a fresh, rewritten and abridged form the story told in *Stranger on the Shore* and *This Life of Grace*, which are both out of print.

A Tear in the Curtain

"This is the history of Russia but in a form that you will not have read it before. It is at the same time objective and intensely personal. It tells is more in a few pages than many more formal accounts manage in a whole volume ... Easy reading, full of insight, and inspiring..." (Dr Michael Bourdeaux)

The Zinoviev Controversy Resolved

"A compellingly researched re-interpretation of one of the most important documents in the history of inter-war British politics. It significantly changes our narrative of the period and has implications that reverberate far beyond the 1920s"
(Stephen Taylor, Professor of History, Durham University)

"An important discovery, which upsets decades of misunderstandings" (Prof. Sir Rick Trainor, Rector , Exeter College, Oxford)

FOR CHILDREN

The Devil's Dance

A story of friendship and trust, eventually victorious over malice and cruelty.

After Life...
Afterlife?

John Symons

SHEPHEARD-WALWYN (PUBLISHERS) LTD

First published in 2021 by
Shepheard-Walwyn (Publishers) Ltd
107 Parkway House, Sheen Lane,
London SW14 8LS
www.shepheard-walwyn.co.uk

British Library Cataloguing in Publication Data
A catalogue record of this book
is available from the British Library

ISBN: 978-0-85683 533 9

Typeset by Alacrity, Chesterfield, Sandford, Somerset

To Judy

Contents

1

The Unasked Question

IN THE LAST MONTHS of 2019 a new virus
emerged in Wuhan in China. No one so far
knows exactly when or how. In early 2020
the virus spread around the world.

With the coronavirus went the invisible
virus of fear, fear of illness, above all fear
of death. No one knew how many people,
previously fit and well, would die, if they
caught it; but the fear, the fear of death, knew
no bounds. By the end of March most of the
population of the world was all but confined
to their own homes and not allowed to come
within six or seven feet of each other when
outside.

2

Desolation
and Consolation

IF YOU DO NOT BELIEVE, do you wish
there were an afterlife? Some people,
perhaps a lot, do not wish for it or even
want to answer the question. Views about the
afterlife are not to be dismissed as a matter of
wishful thinking. For all we know, as many
people wish fervently that that there should be
no afterlife, as wish that there should be.

I am writing this book because I believe
the faith in the afterlife is *true* and I hope to
explain why I do so. When I was a boy, until the
early 1960s, it was quite widely believed. In the
mid-1950s Billy Graham, the American evan-
gelist, conducted a mission, lasting several

weeks, in London, and his ministry reached many parts of the country. Thousands of people are known to have found faith in Christ, a belief in Him for this life and for eternity, beyond this material world, in the afterlife. As large a proportion of the population attended church Sunday by Sunday in England and Scotland in 1958 as in 1918.

When Billy Graham held his next mission ten years later in London in 1966 it was a success and reached the whole country by television relays to local meetings, but the tide had turned against the Christians. The Christian faith in general and in the life to come was waning, and rapidly. Now it is marginal, perhaps even in the church. As someone in the village where my late wife, Judy, and I have attended church services for many years, said, "What churchgoers believe about life after death is usually no different from the rest of the village. They don't believe in it." Although he exaggerated, he was on to something important. Church leaders and believers rarely speak of heaven.

There was a time when many, even most, people believed in an afterlife. Only thirty five years ago, in 1985, a distinguished Soviet political analyst and historian told me privately that the Soviet leaders would never launch a first strike of nuclear weapons against the West. They knew that the West would respond in kind, and the Soviet leaders, all of them atheists and materialists, feared death and had no hope of a life beyond the grave in God's presence. They believed that in the West there was still an active faith in God and in the life of the world to come. Amazingly, the Soviet leaders believed that that faith made it possible for Western leaders, in confidence, to launch a first strike against them. On such matters, my Russian friend always spoke to me openly and in full confidence when we were alone because he knew me to be a Christian, a religious believer. He knew that I would understand and take seriously some of his beliefs which others might regard as naive.

Whether or not there was such a belief in God and the afterlife in the West at that time during the Cold War among our Western leaders, who knows? However that may be, by 2020 everything had changed among the people of the developed Western world. The fear of the coronavirus and of death was deeply felt and palpable. Faith in God was found in a tiny minority; the majority did not share it and was indifferent or hostile to the faith.*

This book is written for that vast majority, people who have no expectation of the life of the world to come. This is what impels me to write. Certainly I have no pretension that I could *persuade* anyone of this truth. I am not that much of a fool. I am a layman, a nonentity, but I have one advantage. Since I was twenty-three years old, God has given me plenty of time to think about death. It was at that age that the doctor told me that the long-standing

---

* In 1983, 66 per cent of the British population identified themselves as Christians; in 2018 the figure was 38 per cent. Those identifying themselves as "confident atheists" rose from 10 per cent in 1998 to 26 per cent in 2018 (source: British Social Attitudes Survey).

allowed into church buildings, and that was only to satisfy insurance companies.

So, no services, no hopeful address to the faithful, no bells on the greatest day of our year, as Christians.

Compare that with the weekend at the end of lockdown. A bishop emerged and spoke to a big crowd of demonstrators (assuredly including Christians) in Canterbury in support of an important social and political matter. In London the bells of churches rang out to mark the third anniversary of the tragedy of the many lives lost in a terrible fire.

One does not need to be a cynic to feel, like my friend in the village, that Christians and church leaders are a good deal more at home with social issues than with the heart of their faith.

Why is this so? My cousin, a Muslim, tells me that it is very different for him and his family. In Islam, the faith in Paradise, the life of the world to come, is, in his words, universal and absolute, among all generations, among believers of various levels of education. In

Britain, there is a terrible fear of death around us. My cousin and his wife sense it and are troubled by it. No less than Islam, the Christian faith has something vital to say about it, to free us of the fear, to give us confidence and hope. I believe that non-believers will also find it of interest.

The gap is obvious to everyone. How is it to be dealt with? Those who believe must speak now and speak clearly.

3
A Testimony

A YEAR BEFORE my father died, Judy and I got married. By then we had known each other for six years, for most of the time as simple friends. Judy was an exceptional person. We had a rare marriage. One stranger said privately to a friend of ours after we had spent a couple of hours with her, "Together, they radiate happiness." It was true. Another stranger, on a holiday tour of Sicily, said to us "Where does the happiness come from?" Judy and I were blessed.

Just three days short of the fiftieth anniversary of our first meeting, the doctor told us that Judy had myeloma, cancer of the bone marrow. "There is no cure but it can be held off." It was held off the four years. Judy died five days before what would have been her seventy-fourth birthday in May 2019.

In all those years – the years of my father's illness, the happy and healthy decades that Judy and I had together, the three years at the end of her life that my mother spent in hospital, then more happy and healthy years for Judy and me, and finally during the four and a quarter years when we were pursued by Judy's cancer – we had a lot of time to ponder this life and its meaning, if any.

In my testimony to Judy and to all that I owe her at her funeral, I said something about this. It was a wonderful service on a beautiful day – Ascension Day – the thirtieth of May 2019.

Judy Symons
My testimony to her,
Ascension Day, 30th May 2019
Judy and I are very grateful to all those who have supported the two of us, above all in prayer, over these many months of her cancer. It has been a special bond, a link like no other.

This was sometimes very costly. Judy reflected God's fairness. At her confirmation the Bishop gave her the words, "I can do all things in Christ who strengthens me."

Judy thought the best of people, and gave them the benefit of the doubt. She always consciously looked for what was good and true, and to do what was right. She always sought forgiveness and reconciliation, and prayed and worked for it among those who were at odds with each other.

She is a remarkable person. I can hardly use the past tense of her. I truly believe that, just as Judy is now blessed to be in the presence of God in our Lord Jesus Christ, so mysteriously He is blessed to have her in His nearer presence.

Judy made three homes for us, peaceful, cosy refuges, first in Ely for a year, then in London and finally here. She loved gardening, and created beautiful gardens.

Judy also loved making music, playing the piano and singing. She was a gifted pianist, and at the age of seventeen was awarded a distinction in her Grade Eight exam. She played the music and ran a small choir at our church in Lewisham. She loved being a member of the Etchingham Singers. It was a sad Sunday when, in July 2017, she found here at St Mary's that she could no longer sing soprano.

And here at St Mary's she was a church warden for four fulfilling years, at the urgent request of the Vicar, Tim Mills. She did the job well, and gave it half her time during those years. I am very proud of what she did then, so happily.

It was in those days when Judy was warden that our dear friend Rose Chavasse said to me, "Everybody loves Judy. Judy's a wonderful girl." As usual, Rose got it right.

Judy was diagnosed with cancer just three days short of the fiftieth anniversary of our first meeting. By then, we had had many happy years together, and tremendous fun and uproarious laughter, as well as adventurous travels, mountain walks and cultural explorations. Of course, we had had sad times, *like everyone. We had, I say, many happy years, but our last years since the diagnosis have been our happiest and closest, and we were very close before that. In the famous words, we have experienced a severe mercy.*

A great friend said to us, "You were lucky to find each other." He is right. Judy and I saved each other. We both knew that and often spoke of it together.

All that gives good grounds for happiness, but there is more to say. All the years Judy and I have known each other, we have been Christians. Steadily, Judy and I came to have a deep belief in the life of the world to come. This belief came from thought and experience, the head used most rigorously, as well as from the heart; but it was God's gift, too. We came to believe in the life of the world to come at a time when we were fit and well, happy and fulfilled, when no sane person could have accused us of wishful thinking. It deserves to be explained.

In the years that He walked this earth before His crucifixion and resurrection, Jesus was recognised by those who knew Him as more than an individual person, however gifted and dedicated. Those who knew Him best acknowledged Him as the supreme representative of Israel, God's chosen people, and of all mankind.

This humble person spoke of Himself as "the Son of Man", the One in Whom God's will was and would be accomplished, through self-sacrifice and death and then glorious triumph, so incorporating in Himself all those who accepted that they were part of Him. Jesus spoke of God as His Father, addressing Him in prayer in an intimate way. He was crucified and rose from the dead.

Jesus lives for all eternity, with those who love Him as His limbs or branches, to share His glory as children of the Father, again for all eternity. Because Jesus lives, death cannot appal us. We belong to Jesus, now and forever.

As Judy and I know, and as my beloved parents each said to me urgently in the months before their deaths, "Everything depends on our Lord Jesus Christ. Everything depends on Jesus."

Thirty years ago Judy and I bought our cottage down here. In those days Judy was working a four day week at school. On Friday she used to pack up in London and drive down in our Morris Minor, have a walk with our dog Jumble, have tea, light the Rayburn, and get things ready for the weekend. She would collect me at the station after my work.

On His last evening with His disciples, Jesus told them: "I am going on ahead to pre-pare a place for you, and in my Father's house, there will be many rooms for you to stay." Judy and I trust that, in God's mercy, one of those places prepared by Our Lord Jesus Christ is for us, for her and for me.

Judy and I believe that, as Jesus taught, when we married each other, so long ago, God created something new, one flesh, a closeness that grew deeper over the years, in good times and in bad, and above all in these last sad, joyful and happy years.

So, Judy has now gone on ahead, to be with

*the Lord and to pray and rejoice in Him, and,
in God's mercy, to prepare a place for me to
join her, the place prepared for us together, by
our Lord Jesus Christ, on whom everything
depends.*

Since Judy's death God has blessed me, and
others, by the presence of Judy, in the spirit, in
their lives. In this life, we are body-and-spirit;
after death, in God's mercy, we are spirit, both
in His presence and, it seems, available for
Him to use to comfort and help others in His
service. In this way, Judy is nearer to me now
(I feel her presence as I write this) than I can
be to her.

One day, it came to me in my prayers that,
in a mysterious way, not only am I mourning
the loss of Judy, but she is also mourning
for me. Mourning means many things, but it
includes "longing for". I felt led to believe that
Judy longs for me, in God's near presence, as
I long for her. How can this be, when God is
"all-in-all" for each of us? Only because, in our
marriage, God made us one being in our Lord

my firm conviction, reached on other grounds, of the life of the world to come. May it encourage or strengthen your belief, as God has used it for me. I will report what happened as clearly as I can.

On the previous Thursday Judy's dear cousin, Fiona, visited us. She and Judy had a good talk. Later Dr Robertson called on us at home because by then it was clear that Judy would soon die. He was very kind. Late that evening, Judy fell in the bathroom, and from that time she had to stay in bed. We had extended our small cottage when Judy retired so that we could live downstairs, with doors big enough for a wheel chair. It was a great blessing. Judy never needed a wheelchair.

The nurses from the hospice came on Friday and Saturday morning and made Judy comfortable so that she was able to spend her last few days in bed at home. For a while, with all the coming and going, I was unsure whether I would be able to cope. I feared that Judy might have to be moved to the hospice. As quiet and calm returned and our routine re-established itself, I felt reassured that all would be well. It was a great relief. To die at home was Judy's great desire, and mine.

On Sunday two of Judy's friends of fifty-five years, from their years as teachers together, Ros and Mary, visited us; Judy was aware of their visit and smiled at them. Four other friends from church also called on us and saw Judy and prayed at her bedside.

On Monday Judy's sister, Jane, and nephew, Harry, came.

On Monday night Mary came back and sat with Judy so that I was able to get some sleep upstairs, for the first time for four nights. The nurses came in the middle of the night to attend to Judy, and Mary found it all but impossible to wake me. Mary went home after breakfast, and our routine re-established itself for the last few hours.

At eight o'clock, after my supper, I went into our bedroom to sit with Judy. Over the next ten minutes, her life in *this* world drew to its close. Once or twice I gently moistened Judy's lips. She took three gasps at the end and was gone.

In those ten minutes together Judy and I were going through the greatest mystery in the world. We had no one else to think about, to worry about, or to consider. In those minutes, Judy, the person Judy, the spirit of Judy, completed her separation from the body in which she had lodged for the seventy-three years and three hundred and sixty days of her life on earth.

A month after Judy's death I visited Dr Robertson. I told him that I was afraid that the final drops of water that I used to refresh her lips had drowned her. He explained that this was not so. I told him that something (one would call it "physical", I suppose) had been happening to Judy as Monday passed in the hours before her death that I wished to mention to him.

I now understand that what I sensed on the Monday before I lost Judy in this world was an indication that in some way Judy, the heart of Judy, the real Judy, her spirit, her person, her self (call it what you will) was gently separating from her body to be with God forever in the

34

world to come. It is an amazing gift from God that he granted me to sense something of this.

I believe that God does for each of us what is necessary for or needed by that particular person. What He did for Judy and for me was done privately for us, and He will do for you what you need. Wait on Him all the time so that He has the chance to do it.

And this is the heart of the matter, the most important question that any of us faces. Are we, or are we not, created by God to live for ever, first in this world and then in His nearer presence in the life of the world to come?

There is no middle way with this question. Which answer is true?

5
The Heart of
the Matter

IT IS ONLY FAIR to tell you something of
what my belief in the life of the world to
come amounts to.

Do I truly mean life after death, after the
decomposition of our bodies in the earth or in
fire? Yes, I do.

Do I mean your individual life, Judy's life,
my life? Yes, I do.

My experience testifies to this and I believe
that my reasons, explained later in the book,
support this belief.

My life has been easy in many ways. I have
had saints and heroes for a wife and parents,
but with enough sadness to echo and share

St Paul's sentiment, "If for this life only we have put our hope in Christ, we are of all people the most to be pitied."

Jesus made it clear to His followers that reaching this eternal goal is no easy matter. He tells us to build our lives on the rock, not on sand, to take the narrow road through the narrow gate to be with Him and to avoid the wide road and gate that leads only to destruction.[1] He tells us that we must bid farewell to all that is ours in the world – parents, brothers, sisters, kinsfolk, friends and our material goods.[2]

In his image of the division of humanity at the end of time, He says that we will be separated between sheep, who have shown others love and mercy, and goats, who have not; a final destiny in the hands of God.[3] Yet Jesus also tells us that His yoke is light and His burden easy and He bids us come to Him to find our rest.[4] Mysteriously, our future in eternity as

---

[1] Gospel of St Matthew chapters 5-7.

[2] Gospel of St Luke chapter 14, verse 33.

[3] St Matthew chapter 25, verses 31-46.

[4] St Matthew chapter 11, verses 28-30.

individuals depends both on our effort and on God's working it out in us equally – the two blades of a pair of scissors, each of the two essential. In St Paul's words, we are to "work out our salvation in fear and trembling", and to recognise that even our wishing to do so, let alone our managing to do so, is entirely God's doing.[5]

This is a personal matter, so I must speak directly. What do I dare to look forward to, in God's mercy, after my own death?

First, I do not take anything for granted. Yet this is what I hope for, what gives the point to my going on living now. I believe that in God's presence and mercy I shall be reunited fully with Judy as individual spirits – even more fully than in this life, linked together in Christ, individuals yet also the two of us as one being. That unity is what Jesus said of married couples and it is not to be put asunder.[6] It is God's creation for eternity when it is freely chosen by man and wife in Him.

---

[5] St Paul, Letter to the Philippians chapter 2, verse 13.

[6] Gospel of St Mark chapter 10, verse 8.

Do I mean that, in God's mercy, Judy and I will again be one being, as well as individuals, as our marriage in Christ made us in this world? Yes, I do. I believe that just as God granted that I should see Judy on her way as she left this life, so God will, in His mercy, grant that she should receive me into the life of the world to come.

Judy and I enjoyed great happiness in this life, but also much sadness and trouble. Both of us are sinners. Each of us made mistakes, sometimes serious mistakes – sins – but eventually we acknowledged our mistakes and repented and forgave each other.

One of the things that Judy said to me, urgently, in her last years when she was afflicted by cancer, was "Remember how horrible I can be!" She knew that I sometimes see people through rose-tinted spectacles and sometimes blame myself for things that were someone else's fault. She was warning me not to idealise her. Both of us could be horrible, and we knew it. I am a sinner as was Judy in this life. We both knew it.

Perhaps now, in the life to come, she is totally free of all the effects of her sins and of mine which affected her, as I hope we shall be when we are together again, yet somehow conscious of them so that we see what would have been our life apart from them. Perhaps the pain arising from that God-given vision is the heart of the doctrine of purgatory, which we must go through, in God's loving mercy, to be wholly His as He, and we, wish. So I trust and believe that finally, in the life of the world to come, all these sadnesses and pains and troubles will be like the tears that God promises to wipe away from our eyes, over and gone.

Judy once said to me, in the 1980s, "It's Jumble who makes us a family." Jumble was our first border terrier, with Sam his brother who died as a puppy of nine months. They were followed in our lives by Bracken, and later by Daniel. As Judy said, they made us a family, dear in our hearts. They made us what we are. I believe that each of them will be there with us, in God's loving mercy, in the life of the world to come. As the Orthodox Church teaches, they do not sin and are "in Eden", so they will be with us.

Judy and I were blessed in our parents. I believe that they, too, will be there, that we shall be joyfully reunited. For example, we shall be reunited with my father, totally my father yet wholly free of the Huntington's disease that slowly ravaged him for years; and with my mother, wholly untroubled by all the anxiety that she bore because of my father's illness and their fears for the health of my brother and me. We shall see Judy's parents unaffected by the sadness that troubled them because of their long wartime separation, when one of them was in England and the other in the Army in India and the Middle East.

It will be a wonderful state to be in. Judy used to say to me, when we had difficult problems to resolve, "We get there in the end!" In God's mercy, we will get to that state in the end.

But it will not be solely a *state*. We shall be active. What grounds can I have for believing this? I will explain my reasons in the next chapter, but I will add the following here.

We must ask ourselves "How will I know that I am there, in the presence of God, for all eternity?" For me it would be so if the One receiving us were clearly the One who, in the tension and hostility of Holy Week, spotted the elderly widow putting her mite into the collection tray and then told those around Him that she had given more than anyone with wealth to give. [7] The burden, the yoke, laid upon us by that Saviour, is indeed light and kind. There, in God's mercy, may we find our home, for all eternity.

God is Lord of time and space, their creator. He will be able to allow us, together, to live again and review our life together. He will, I believe, let Judy and me live through our life as it would have been if we had not ourselves made mistakes; and as it would have been if the mistakes of others had not damaged our lives. That will be a gift indeed. He will show us where we went wrong when it was in our power to take the right decision, and if ever, truly against the odds which we faced in some test-

---

[7] St Luke chapter 21, verses 1-4.

42

ing circumstance, we did the right thing. That, too, will be a mercy. Who can doubt that the Father of mercies will allow us those blessings, incorporated, as we are, in His beloved Son? Nothing is too great and too loving for Him to wish to grant us.

I am expressing myself in simple, homely, naïve, and direct terms but I can do no better. Every day, I try while still in this world to be there, in the Lord, where Judy now is. A friend told me that she was angry with God because of losing her, but I cannot bring myself to begrudge Judy to God. It is as if I know how He feels, wanting to have her in His nearer presence, just as I do. It will be so for me, God grant, and perhaps quite soon. Until then I am "marking time", an important matter in Army drill which permits two individual soldiers or units to join together in a clear and decisive way. I dare to believe that, mysteriously, Judy is also marking time, yet active in God's presence as I am here, until we are reunited in God's nearer presence. What joy it will be.

While Judy had cancer, she pressed me to

have a day off every week, and on those days one or other of her friends used to visit her to keep her company. In her good periods, they could go on an outing, for lunch or to visit a garden. I used to go to our old house in London and have a very quiet time or meet a friend for lunch. It worked well: Judy, too, needed a change! I recall one evening when I arrived home earlier than Judy was expecting me. I glimpsed her through the window for a moment, and then she looked up and saw me. I shall never forget the look on her face: I feel unworthy of it. My conviction is that, in God's mercy, as we meet again in His nearer presence, spirit and spirit, we shall again experience that joy.

As our late vicar, Michael Simpson, used sometimes to say in his sermons, "The time may be shorter than we think."

6

Three Witnesses

IN THIS BOOK I explain why I believe that we are created by God to live with Him, in His mercy, for ever. I wrote that I believe that, in God's presence, we shall be active in the life of the world to come.

What makes me believe that? Here I want to tell you what happened in the year after Judy's death. I would like to report the evidence from three friends.

The first is Amanda, and what follows is what I told the congregation in our local church on December the first in 2019, six months after Judy's funeral service in that church. We are an ordinary village church, not an eccentric sect. This is the text of my talk at Holy Communion that day.

Advent Sunday, 1ˢᵗ December 2019

Judy and I have always loved Advent. Here is the set of Bible Reading Fellowship notes, *A Feast for Advent* by Delia Smith, which Judy often used and I am using this year.

But this is a special Advent, not only because I am going through it without Judy's physical presence, but for another reason. And it is because of this second reason that I asked for the Vicar's permission to speak these words today.

Advent means the Coming of the Lord, at Christmas and at the end of time. Advent's themes, for its four Sundays, are Heaven, Hell, Death and Judgment. In church the colour of the altar dressing is a solemn purple, to show the magnitude of what is at stake. It is the life of the world to come, beyond this world, beyond this life, in the Communion of the Saints, of all believers, above all in the presence of Jesus Christ, on whom everything depends.

For a moment, but not long, I will speak personally. Every day in my prayers I seek God's presence for the day, and I ask Him, in his mercy, that I may know, may feel Judy with me in the spirit. He has granted me that gift, and I do not take it for granted.

But a hostile critic (I know that is not you) might say that this is just wishful thinking, my fantasy to comfort myself.

This is where what I called the other reason makes this Advent special. It involves a friend of Judy and me who has been our neighbour in London since 2002, Amanda. Amanda died in late September, in her early fifties. She was at Judy's service on Ascension Day.

Amanda was a nurse and a teacher of nurses. She died of cancer. She first got cancer eleven years ago, and was completely cured. That cancer never returned. Then, about two years ago she got another cancer. It was held at bay; there was a remission of a year or so, and then it returned six months ago, just after Judy's funeral.

I got to know Amanda better than Judy did because I was working from home by then, and Amanda, coming off duty, often worked in the garden in the afternoon and we would have a talk. Apart from everything else, we talked about faith and God. Amanda was interested and sympathetic but not a believer.

About a fortnight before her death, when she was in hospital for a few days, Amanda felt very frightened about what was happening to her, especially about her family. The curate, Sarah, who lives opposite us in London, told me at prayers in church about Amanda's fears. Amanda told Sarah when she visited her in hospital how much she wished she had faith and could believe in God but she said she could not. In God's mercy, a day or two after this had happened, I sent Amanda a tiny book, *Enfolded in Love*, excerpts from the *Revelation of Divine Love* by Mother Julian of Norwich.

Then, one morning two or three days later, on Tuesday, from her bed in hospital, Amanda sent me this email:

Dearest John, In a dark moment one recent night, I wondered or felt Judy praying for me or being with me... I have started Lady Julian's prayers and will enjoy a daily read. Fondest love, Amanda.

48

This was five days before Amanda's death. I replied as follows:

Dearest Amanda, Yes, Judy is praying for you and for me, and for many others, praise God for her. Fondest love, which you know comes from Judy and me, John.

Two days passed.

Sarah wrote the following account for me of what happened on Friday.

As I sat with Amanda (this was two days before her death) she told me of an experience she had had in the night... She had experienced the presence of God all around her and wanted to let God in but she just felt so sick. Amanda said she then saw Judy there with her, that Judy was praying for her. Amanda described how she *felt* all our prayers, not just appreciated them but *felt* them, *was held* by them. She believed, and wanted to let God in. I offered to anoint her with oil and pray for her and with her, which she accepted with tears in her eyes. As I prayed for her and anointed her, her whole body relaxed and I believe she received the peace from God which she needed.

On that day, Friday, after Sarah had visited her, Amanda telephoned me, here in Sussex, and left me a message. She told me that she was treasuring the little book of Lady Julian's writings and found them "beautiful, special". She referred to the words about God as "Maker, Lover and Keeper", very special to her, she said. "Look after yourself, John," she said, her last words to me.

Amanda died on Sunday. Sarah wrote: "When I saw her on Sunday she still had that peace... She was ready for her home in God's embrace."

Thanks be to God. Amanda died in the Lord.

I am full of confidence that, along with Judy, Amanda is now praying for her family, for Sarah and for me, and for so many others, in the nearer presence of the Lord.

This is the only public event in my life which I regard as a miracle, God intervening or interfering in the natural, material world. What does it show? Many things, but I wish to emphasise just one. It is never too late for God.

By His grace, He catches us as we fall between the bridge and the river beneath us.

Remember: Heaven, Hell, Death, Judgment. The life of the world to come. In my mind there is no doubt that, in the spirit, through God's grace, Judy, – Judy, my wife, whom you knew for nearly twenty years – was present to Amanda, was with her, just as I, in God's mercy, have sensed Judy with me.

Jesus died and rose. He defeated death and sin. Amanda died in the Lord. Like Judy, my beloved wife, Amanda, our dear friend, is now alive in Christ in the life of the world to come. It is a great truth, one for each of us to lay hold of and never give up. This Advent we look to the Risen Lord Jesus Christ, – Jesus on whom everything depends, and with whose love it is never too late.

I have told some friends about all this. When I told Penny and John, friends for over fifty years, they said, "Of course, it's exactly the sort of thing that Judy would have done!"

The second witness is Justina.

Justina's testimony is to an event in February 2020, five or so months after Judy came to Amanda on her deathbed. Again, what Judy did was God's response to a person in spiritual need (this time it was me): He used Judy in His service. This is how it happened.

Years ago, in 2010, I met Justina, a writer and teacher of writing, at an Arvon Foundation writing course in Scotland. We kept in touch by texts but had not met since 2012, but Justina and I have remained prayer partners.

One day, in February 2020, I sent Justina a text which must have worried her, causing her to think that I was in danger of losing the equilibrium that God, in His mercy, has given me since I lost Judy. This is what she wrote:

> John, you are doing so well. I will pray.
>
> I hope I'm not speaking out of turn.
>
> A couple of weeks ago when I was worrying about you, I had a very strong sense of Judy, through you, with a message:
>
> "It's not your job to *worry* about John. You don't have to worry as I have got him so tightly in my care."

The message that God asked Judy to pass to Justina gave me so much comfort and encouragement, both in its own right, and because it was so congruent with all that I have felt since I lost Judy: Judy with me, in the Spirit, day by day, in God's mercy.

The third witness is Fiona.

Fiona is Judy's youngest cousin; they are more like sisters than cousins, although separated in age by almost ten years. They share a birthday. Over the years, Fiona, and her husband Ken and Judy and I had celebrated their birthday jointly, often with a walk or picnic on the South Downs. Fiona read the words of the Bible at Judy's funeral service.

Both Fiona and Judy had been greatly strengthened in their Christian faith by their Uncle Alan's witness to Christ. He had been a prisoner of war of the Japanese on the Burma railway for three years and had been tortured. He put this terrible period of his life behind him and bore no ill will. Uncle Alan took Judy and me to the Oberammergau Passion Play in

1980, with a walking holiday to follow. Fiona says that she owes her Christian faith to Uncle Alan's witness to Christ. She was with him at the end of his life and witnessed his raising his head and acknowledging the One who came to receive him as the end came.

On the day following their joint birthday in May in 2020, Fiona told me:

> I felt Judy was very close to me last night. She kissed me on my forehead as I was about to go to sleep. She is my guardian angel and always has been. I am so grateful that she has always been beside me in my life, guiding and cheering me on. I'm grateful she's still there.

In our Lord Jesus Christ, Judy was active in His service that night.

For my part, I had a bad night, with sad dreams. But one of them led to my waking with the new realisation: "Judy is mourning me, too." God gave me those words in my prayers.

How can it be that, in the nearer presence of the Lord, Judy is *mourning*? In a way, why should she bother about me at all? Yet she does. My *In Memoriam* notice on the anniversary of her death included the words *The two shall become one.* St Paul wrote those words to the early Christians at Ephesus to describe the marriage of a Christian husband and wife.[8]

My testimony to the year after Judy's death is of her life as the person Judy in the spirit in the Lord, and of her care both for others and for me.

As for me, an Antiochian Orthodox priest, Father Alexander, expressed it briefly and clearly. "She is nearer to you than you can *now* be to her," he said. In our shared life, married for just short of forty-eight years, as body-and-spirit, spiritual persons created by God through our parents in bodies, we could each be as close to the other as the other could be to us. Judy is now in the spirit: the person Judy is now pure spirit, in God's presence, but in His mercy, she is able to be present to me. She can also be with others.

We, who are left, still struggle on, in this "vale of tears". I am tempted to say "encum-

---

[8] St Paul, Letter to the Ephesians chapter 5, verse 31, RSV translation.

bered with a physical body" but God loves matter, his material creation; He loves us as bodily spirits. But in His will, the original objective was that in this form we should love Him wholly: so it was in the beginning. Now, still in this life, I cannot experience Judy's presence with me as fully as she can have me in her presence, and keep me in her loving care, under God.

So, I feel it is a wonderful mercy that Judy, in God, mourns the fact that we suffer this temporary separation and, like me, hopes for the day when we shall be together as pure spirits in the love of God in our Lord Jesus Christ, in the communion, the shared fellowship of all Christ's people, in the life of the world to come.

Secondly, Father Alexander said, "In heaven you will be *even more* to each other than you could be in this world." In this world as spirits-in-bodies we were so important to each other, but we made mistakes, we were sometimes pressed on all sides, not valuing each other as we should have done. I speak for myself, but Judy felt the same. In the world to come, in

God's nearer presence and mercy, we know that the time for tears and regrets is past. We can be fully to each other what God called us to be. It is this that I now long for, it is this for which Judy now mourns, knowing what I am going through as we await what will be our experience, the two of us for ever one in the Lord.

In the meantime, God has granted me these signs that Judy is still active in His service, as she was in this life. They are the only public things that I have known in my life which I regard as miracles, events which happened to people whom I know directly and personally and whom I trust and trust for good reasons; events which cannot be explained in terms of material cause and effect, that is, in each case, God interfered in the natural material world.

These three events, three miracles involving Amanda, Justina and Fiona, may well leave unbelievers cold and unaffected. How can it be otherwise? I sympathise with and understand their reaction. They can always put down what happened to the state of the brain of those to whom it happened, Amanda, Justina and Fiona, or to my wishful thinking. They are committed, are they not, to explaining everything in materialistic terms? Of course, they do not think of their own explanations in materialistic terms: they cannot consistently do so. Their philosophy saws off the branch on which they are sitting. There is more to be said about that in a later chapter, but let us first turn to the substance of the Christian faith, the truth of which alone makes sense of the miracles that Amanda, Justine and Fiona and I have experienced, through God's goodness.

7

Heart and Mind

EVERYONE KNOWS that you can never change anyone's political views in an argument or discussion, if you are foolish enough to try. We found that to be true in the long public row about leaving the European Union. "Row" is the only word to do it justice; it was no debate or discussion or conversation. Both sides sensed the impotence of reason and so made use of fear. Perhaps the three and a half years of fear, from the referendum in June 2016 to the final Parliamentary decision at end of 2019, following the general election in December, ploughed the field in which the seeds of the fear of coronavirus could grow so luxuriantly.

It is even more difficult to change one's own

or another person's religious beliefs or practices solely by reason. Reason plays an important part, but only with time and experience. I am not fool enough to believe that I can convince you by reasons and arguments.

Experience is vital. Suppose for a moment, if you are not a religious believer, that God loves us and is active. Believers sense this from their personal experience. Does it not stand to reason that He would be using every chance to reach out to us, to let us meet Him, supremely in His activity in Jesus, in His identity with Jesus, but also in our ordinary life? Of course, we can refuse to meet Him; or meet Him and then turn away, at least for a while. It is difficult, but perhaps not impossible, to turn away for ever.

In the early years after the Second World War, Kenneth Clark, art historian and scholar, the Director of the National Gallery during the War, and in the late 1960s famous for his *Civilisation* programmes on television, met God in Florence. He wrote that he had a religious experience in the Church of San

Lorenzo, not, he believed, connected with the harmonious beauty of the architecture there. He said that, for a few minutes, his whole body was irradiated by a kind of heavenly joy, far more intense than anything he had known before and that this state of mind lasted for several months. He commented that, wonderful though it was, it posed an awkward problem in terms of action. He wrote that his life was far from blameless and that he would have to reform. His family would think he was going mad. "Perhaps, after all, it was a delusion, for I was in every way unworthy of receiving such a flood of grace. Gradually the effect wore off, and I made no effort to retain it. I think I was right; I was too deeply embedded in the world to change course. But that I had felt 'the finger of God' I am quite sure, and although the memory of this experience has faded, it still helps me to understand the joy of the saints."[9]

---

[9] Kenneth Clark, *The Other Half: A Self Portrait*, John Murray (Publishers) Ltd, 1977.

Lord Clark may have believed, for a while, that his reasons, so clearly, frankly and disarmingly expressed here, had saved him from changing course. But God did not give up – He clearly never does – and ten days or so before his death in May 1983, he yielded to God's love and received the sacraments of the church. His widow, herself a believer, said that she believed that her husband's decision had been "maturing most of his life" (*The Times*, 15th October 1983, including a short interview with Lady Clark following Lord Clark's memorial service).

This astonishing and moving story shows how God seeks to meet us and leaves us to use our minds to decide whether we wish to continue in His company. It is also a troubling story. Who can tell what God would have had in store, in this world, for him and us, if Kenneth Clark had yielded himself to God totally in San Lorenzo? I cannot doubt that God would have revealed the answer to that question to Lord Clark in the life of the world to come. It is impertinent to go further and reflect on what Lord Clark's reaction might have been. We must think in those terms only of mistakes we ourselves have made when *we* turned away from God. May Lord Clark rest in peace.

In the same sudden way, perhaps, God met Saul of Tarsus, later St Paul, on the road from Jerusalem to Damascus where he was travelling in order further to persecute the infant Church. Saul was wholeheartedly converted there and then. As he relates in his letter to the Galatian Christians, written perhaps fifteen years later, he went away to spend three years in Arabia, and then Damascus, to use his mind and heart to come to terms with what God had done to him in that meeting. Then he was ready to go to Jerusalem to see St Peter and other apostles.[10]

If God gives us enough time in this life, this is often how we change and come to Him. Our mind and our heart work together.

Perhaps you have never felt God tugging at your heart or mind or touching you or speaking

---

[10]   St Paul, Letter to the Galatians chapter 1, verses 13-20.

to you. You are in the same boat as many others, but there is nothing to keep you there. It is possible to give ourselves time to see whether, really, God is doing that for us, yet so far we have not noticed Him. It is all too easy to fail to notice Him. He does not always push Himself on us.

How can we give ourselves this chance?

There are two ways known to me (I expect that there are others), and the story of how Archbishop Antony Bloom found his faith and of the consequences of that for other people illustrates the first.

Antony Bloom was the son of a diplomat in the Russian Foreign Service, in Tsarist Russia early in the twentieth century before Lenin and Trotsky seized power for the Bolsheviks in late 1917. When his father was serving in Persia, Antony's parents became worried about him. They saw that he had a brilliant, original mind – he was in his teens – but he was wayward, careless of people, and an atheist. His father confronted him about his behaviour and attitudes and reminded him of the Christian heritage of his family. He challenged him to read one, just one, of the gospels of Christ's life, death and resurrection in the New Testament. For peace and quiet, Antony agreed. He tells us that he chose to read St Mark's gospel, because it is the shortest, but he read it alone, in quiet and with attention.

Archbishop Antony told this story many times, because what then happened changed his life. He began to read casually but became more and more gripped by the Gospel as he read it. He tells us that as time passed, he became convinced that the One of whom he was reading was there with him, in the room; that, if he raised his eyes from the pages of the book, he would see Jesus there with him.

Antony Bloom was made new in Christ; he was changed. With the coming to power of the Bolsheviks, he found himself an exile in Paris along with thousands of other Russians. He was impoverished but somehow managed to qualify as a doctor, while working as a volunteer in the Russian Orthodox Church there. He became a priest and worked in the Resistance during the German occupation, from 1940 to 1945. Soon afterwards, as a priest, he was posted by the Church to London, where he led the Orthodox congregation, first as priest and then as bishop and finally as Metropolitan Archbishop. So great was the respect in which he was held that in his last years he was seriously considered for the position of Patriarch, the supreme leader, in Moscow, of the Russian Orthodox Church.

Throughout his years in London, Antony Bloom had a great influence on Christians in all the churches. He was a loyal Orthodox but not sectarian, always speaking for the Jesus who came to him, in Persia, as, reluctantly and dutifully, he read St Mark's gospel to satisfy his father.

This is the first way, then, if we dare, to give ourselves a chance to notice God when He approaches us. It is to read the Bible, especially the gospels. It pays to read them again and again, without ceasing, in different translations.

It may take a long time to grasp what God is

telling us of Himself. Antony Bloom was blessed in his first reading of St Mark, but God has His own way with each of us. The thing to do is to read the gospels time after time. Some passages which are unclear at an early reading become clearer, and some passages clear on a first reading get more difficult. The thing is, never to give up. The whole point is to grasp, if we may, the nature, the actions, the works, the sense of purpose, the power, the love, the gentleness, the severity, and the mercy of the gospels' extraordinary central figure. It takes a lifetime to begin to take this in, but we can grasp enough, in time or quickly, to find ourselves held by Him and to realise that this compulsion we come to feel is for our own good, for our salvation, in time and in eternity.

The second way is to look out for people who have been changed by encountering God: not creepy, weird, sanctimonious people, but people who are different from us in a good way, in whom we find something better than there is in us, perhaps something to do with God. One way to find some such people is to go to church, and to look out for anyone like this. Most churches have a few if we can bring ourselves to go there. It will be a good sign if we can do that: it will mean that we do not think of ourselves as the cat's whiskers; that we sense that we are in need of something, someone, God. God often then makes use of that chance, that humility of which we had not imagined ourselves capable.

The person, or people (if we are lucky enough to find more than one), to help us in this way, may well be completely unlike us. They may well have no idea that they are helping us. Again, this will be a good sign. We can be, they can be, completely unselfconscious. God can somehow act more freely, in a deeper way when we totally forget ourselves.

All of this may well take a long time, perhaps many years. No one but God, and Antony Bloom now in the life of the world to come, can know why or how God acted so quickly, so urgently in his case. All that matters is that God did it and that Antony Bloom responded. We are dealing with the most important thing in the world that any of us can face: what God created us for, redeemed us for – to be with Him in the communion of those who have been saved by Him in Jesus.

Jesus himself told us how important this is. Imagine a person who finds a priceless treasure hidden in a field. The person longs to have the prize and so sells everything he has in order to buy it and own it for ever. [11] How much more is this true of our life in all eternity? We must use all the resources we have to be with Him, safe in His love.

A few days after Judy's death it was necessary for me to register her death in Lewes, the county town of East Sussex. It was a terrible prospect, and I dreaded it, but I decided to go alone, but for the company of Judy, in her spirit. I reached the friendly village of Ringmer. Judy and I had often pulled the car into a small car park there and watched a few overs of cricket on the village green beside the road through the village. We used to take advantage

---

[11] St Matthew chapter 14, verses 44-8.

of the public toilets there. Feeling nervous on this morning on my way to Lewes, I pulled in to use them. They were closed for renovation. I walked into the library next door and asked a lady there if I could use the library's facilities. She was setting up a room for a group meeting. On my way out, I had a word with her. What was the group? A bible reading and prayer group, she said. What passages were they to study that morning? The passages from Jesus' Sermon on the Mount in St Matthew's Gospel, "Seek ye first the Kingdom of God... Let not your hearts be troubled."[12]

God spoke to me through that kind lady. He told me to go ahead in faith to register Judy's death. He told me that, with my loss of Judy in this world, there must be no end to the effort to get closer to Jesus day by day, that I must give myself more to Him, and that the end to this in this world would come when, in His mercy, He took me in my turn. There could be nothing more important.

---

[12] St Matthew chapter 6, verses 33-4.

8

Mind and Heart

T HE GREATEST ARGUMENT for the
Christian faith is not a matter of
abstract reasoning, but the person
of Jesus. St John's gospel calls Jesus the
"Word" of God, the "Reason" of God, that
which makes sense of everything else, and
that Reason is a Person. In this way, His person
is an argument.

St Paul tells us that the whole Being of God
dwells in Jesus in bodily form. The beginning
and the end of time, everything is encompassed
in Him. It takes some grasping: we can never
understand it. Yet as, time and again, perhaps
over many years, we grow near Him as He
reaches out to us as we constantly read the
gospels and pray, He comes to seem the only

answer, and this happens to people who seem otherwise sane, reasonable and likeable.

When Judy was ill, three long dead Christian writers, of whom I previously knew little, helped me.

One was William Temple (1881-1944). Dr Temple was the son of an Archbishop of Canterbury, Frederick Temple, who in his turn held that post in the Second World War. Earlier, he had been a headmaster of a big school, a vicar in the West End of London, Bishop of Manchester and Archbishop of York. He was a philosopher as well as a theologian and yet his way of summing up Christianity was to say "Christianity is Christ". In the 1960s people remembered attending mission services when he used that phrase. It cannot be bettered.

The other two writers who helped me were Edwyn Bevan (1870-1943) and John Stocks (1882-1937). Both of them are almost forgotten whereas there is naturally still an interest in William Temple because of his prominent public life in the Church hierarchy and in the country in the 1930s and the Second World War. William Temple and John Stocks were good friends from their time together at Oxford University as undergraduates and later philosophy tutors there. Edwyn Bevan was respected and admired by William Temple but I do not know whether Edwyn Bevan and John Stocks knew each other.

All three men wrote and taught over the four decades until 1940. A striking virtue shared by all three is that they tried hard to do full justice to the strength of the reasons and arguments of those with whom they disagreed. They did this without trimming their own Christian faith, beliefs and convictions.

Edwyn Bevan was an historian of the ancient world – the Middle East, Greece and Rome. He was also a philosopher and, like William Temple, gave the Gifford lectures on religion in the 1930s.

John Stocks was a philosopher at Oxford, then at Manchester University, for twenty years; and at the end of the 1930s he was made Vice Chancellor of Liverpool University.

Within a year, out of the blue, he was dead. He left a widow and three children. His widow, Mary Stocks, like her husband, was a convinced Christian. Any reader born like me, just after the Second World War, will remember her and her crisp opinions and clipped pronunciation from the radio. She often appeared on the panel of "Any Questions", a radio programme in those days, the 1950s and early 1960s, not yet given over to politics. Besides that, she gave a series of talks over many years on the Old Testament entitled *Unread Bestseller* (the dry humour is typical of her.) Mary Stocks called her late husband "the best person I have ever known", a tribute indeed for a woman so resolutely unsentimental.

Perhaps you can imagine me during those four years of Judy's illness. I would get out of bed ninety minutes before I took Judy a cup of tea. As part of my early prayer time, to set myself up for the day, I used to read a little of these three men's books. I came to envy those who lived in the 1920s and 1930s, although it was a terrible intermission between the world wars, because they had these three men, then at the height of their powers, to teach them; writers full of life, purpose, intelligence, a sense of duty and compassion, prominent yet all convinced, articulate Christians. Who is there now like that? My twenty minutes a day with them at the end of my prayers each morning helped me.

What do they have to teach us of the life of the world to come? What did they teach me? The great lesson they taught me was about the relation between heart and mind, between experience and thought, between feeling and reason in faith. Each of them taught me that lesson in a special way.

It helps us to get at the truth if we read books by great thinkers and scholars from an earlier age. Though they may be affected by the prejudices and assumptions of their own time, it is often easier for us to detect and allow for that than we can throw off the errors of our own age, by which we are ourselves probably deeply infected.

"Christianity is Christ," said Dr Temple:

there is nothing to be added to the faith beyond the person of Jesus Christ. He also said, "The Church is the only organisation that exists solely for the benefit of those outside it." Partly he had it in mind that the Church is to work for the material well-being of outsiders, and he involved himself actively in social matters. He described Christianity as "the most material-istic of all religions". Yet he wrote, with great emphasis, in his Gifford lectures, "The pos-sibility, at least, of eternal life is indispensable to every higher interest of man. Yet in our time, there's an unparalleled absence of concern with the whole subject."[13]

Dr Temple wrote,

There must be an end to such human life as we know on this planet... There might be no end of history, if by history we mean succes-sive events. But there must be an end to *human* history... But the end of history is the complete coming of the Kingdom [of Christ]... The revelation of the Eternal in Jesus Christ forbids us to find the meaning of man's life only, or even chiefly, within

---

[13] *Nature, Man and God,* 1934, p.xxix.

the process of successive events which make up man's terrestrial history. It is to be found in a new creation; not only in a further apprehension of this world order, but in a resurrection to a new order of being and of experience, of which we can only say that so far as we here and now become partakers of the fruits of the Spirit, we are in our degree already realising our citizenship in Heaven.[14]

In the first of his three great books, *Mens Creatrix* (Mind, the Creator), written half way through the First World War, Dr Temple wrote:

The religious man believes in God quite independently of philosophic reasons for doing so; he believes in God because he has a conviction that God has taken hold of him... God is not the conclusion but the starting point... The Christian who is also in any degree a philosopher will not claim that by reason he can irrefragably [unanswerably, irrefutably] establish his faith ... which come[s] to him from the authority of the saints or from his

---

[14] *Christus Veritas* (Christ, the Truth), 1924, pp.210-11.

own specifically religious experience.[15]

In *Christus Veritas,* he notes:

> In popular language, religion is an affair of the heart more than of the head; and the acceptance of its deliverances as decisive for our whole world-view is a leap only justified by its results [p.xii].

But he explains in *Mens Creatrix* that his aim in his book is

> to indicate a real unity between faith and knowledge as something to which we can even now in part attain [p.4].

John Stocks saw matters in the same way. Four years before his early death, he summed up his views on the nature and grounds of religious belief in a series of three lectures given at Durham University. In a striking sentence, he wrote that he was attempting

> to deal only with the intellectual content of religion, and that the specifically religious grounds of religious belief (which are obviously the real grounds) lay necessarily

---

[15] *Mens Creatrix,* 1917, pp.2-4.

outside his direct survey.[16]

At the conclusion of the lectures, he wrote:

> Though an intuitive judgment [religious, moral, aesthetic, philosophical] cannot be proved [like a geometrical theorem] it can make some sort of justification of itself. But the justification always comes in the last resort as a request, addressed to the one who disagrees, that he shall look at the object again more carefully, with special attention to this and that feature of it, and see whether, after such a reinspection, he is not disposed to modify his verdict. Such ... reasons ... are different in logical character equally from the irresistible demonstrations of the mathematician and from the massive probabilities of natural science (p.46).

A couple of years later, in his lectures entitled *Time, Cause and Eternity*, John Stocks went a little further. He argued that the perception that each of us has that events and actions occur one after the other

itself proves that the perceiver is in some

---

[16] *On the Nature and Grounds of Religious Belief,* 1934, p.3.

respect other than temporally successive, which is to say that the perceiver has in some respect non-temporal or timeless being.[17]

He concludes, "The only kind of eternity which has any real significance for religion or for anything else ... is an eternal which is in causal relation with the temporal" (p.159): a conclusion, which in the words of his old friend William Temple, who wrote the introduction to the published lectures, "are familiar elsewhere as the doctrines of creation and eternal life" (p.xi). William Temple and John Stocks, as young men, had each encouraged the other to offer himself for ordination in the Church of England. In 1944, William Temple, as Archbishop, dedicated his famous *Readings in St John's Gospel* to his old friend.

Like the other two writers, Edwyn Bevan shows well how heart and mind, feeling and reason, and experience and thought can work together and be friends in the search for truth,

including the truth of the life of the world to

---

[17] *Time, Cause and Eternity,* 1936, p 143.

come. His friend, Gilbert Murray, Professor of Greek at Oxford, recorded that Bevan valued both the rationalist attitude and what (Professor Murray wrote) he sometimes called "the claims of the God of Israel", while being exceptionally reasonable and determined not to be guided by mere emotion.

Edwyn Bevan wrote:

> Inanimate nature shows an immense preponderance ... over ... the manifestations of life and spirit [which are] confined, so far as observation has yet gone, to an infinitesimal part of space [the Earth] and span of time [human history]... Which of these regions of fact a man takes as being the key to Reality is a matter of personal choice, in which what is deepest in him expresses itself... Those who believe the Reality behind phenomena to be Spirit, to be God, hold that we see the character of that Reality in the manifestations of the human spirit [some higher, some lower] ... and as they rise in the scale ... brighter and purer ... they are for us more perfect manifestations of the Supreme Spirit. For Christians, the human spirit reaches its highest possible

point in Christ, and for that reason the Christian Church believes that in Christ may be seen that for which the whole universe has come into existence ... It is highly improbable that anyone who had no belief in God was ever led to believe in God by any of the standard "proofs" of God's existence... What actually causes anyone to believe in God is direct perception of the Divine."[18]

Edwyn Bevan wrote his last book, *Christians in a World at War,* at the end of 1939, and published it before Churchill became Prime Minister in May 1940. It sums up his reflections on the world, twice at war in his adult life, and on the hope of the life to come. In our own dangerous times, it deserves to be read.

When Edwyn Bevan was writing this book, Stalin was secretly in league with Hitler against us, supplying him with intelligence and material supplies; he invaded Poland both to seize the eastern part of the country for himself, and to help Hitler as his Blitzkrieg slowed. Stalin also seized the Baltic States. His Red Army shook hands and staged a joint parade with the

[18] *Symbolism and Belief,* 1946 edition, pp.342-5.

Nazi troops when they met. Hitler and Stalin were in effect allied against us. The world faced tyranny, misery and disaster under two evil ideologies. By the end of May 1940, Great Britain and her Empire stood alone against the threat. It was a situation which, like ours in 2020 with the coronavirus, in its own way, invites people to face the truth about human life and God. This Edwyn Bevan did. He wrote a great but forgotten book.

He wrote:

> The groups which seem so permanent, in contrast with the perishing individuals – the family, the society, the nation – are merely frames within which during their time on earth human spirits are brought together to be exercised in different kinds of fellowship. The spirits, when their time of learning here is over, pass on, and the frames, when they have served their time, will some day be broken up.
>
> There is only one society, partially manifested on earth, which is an eternal frame, which continues, as a society, in the world beyond death; and that is the Mystical Body

of Christ ... the union of the whole body of those animated by the Spirit of Christ "with the Lord" in perfect fellowship and for ever beyond the reach of death... It is obviously other-worldly... A union of the whole Body of Christ, of all who, in any age, have been animated by His Spirit, could never exist except beyond death and under conditions which, in contrast with the conditions of our space and time, would constitute a wonder-world.[19]

Each of these three writers pointed me to the truth at a time when Judy and I were in great need: the truth that everything is summed up in Christ and that in Him is the hope of the world to come.

Now William Temple, John Stocks and Edwyn Bevan all came from Christian families and were brought up in the faith. Of course, that fact, a happy fact, I believe, in no way diminishes a person's ability to reach an independent judgment or faith. But it is of great

interest to realise that not only those brought up in the faith realise its truth and come to

---

[19] *Christians in a World at War*, 1940, p.96.

know Christ. I have already mentioned the encounter that Antony Bloom had with the risen Christ when, as a teenager, he was an atheist. I do not know whether Lord Clark had a Christian family background before God came to him in silence in the church of San Lorenzo in Florence.

There are two notable examples of prominent lifelong atheists, professors of philosophy, who were radically changed by such an encounter in the last few years of their lives. What happened to them is worth telling here. I do not report these events as an argument for God's existence, but rather as an encouraging sign for me and other believers of what God can do for people who have been hostile to him or have strongly disbelieved in him for many years. Perhaps there is some sort of warning here for all of us about God's implacable love and His patience.

The first of the two was A. J. Ayer, a brilliant and precocious philosopher. In his early days he made his name in 1936 with a book entitled *Language, Truth and Logic*. The book made popular in Britain the philosophy of logical positivism, first expressed by the so-called Vienna School after the First World War. It maintained, among many things, that there was literally no sense, no meaning, in statements about God and His nature and actions, or in moral or aesthetic statements. Why equally abstract philosophical statements of the sort voiced by Professor Ayer should have been regarded by him or anyone else as having meaning was the decisive flaw in this philosophy, as Ayer later acknowledged.

In his later works Ayer watered down the exuberant expression of his views. He never doubted that God did not exist until he was in hospital with pneumonia towards the end of his life, in June 1988. He had an extraordinary near-death experience, about which he wrote in the press.[20] There is a striking quality to the article; he was a wonderful, vivid writer. He was reckoned to have been dead for four minutes. He recorded that he had been confronted with a bright red light, "very painful

---

[20] *Sunday Telegraph*, 28th August 1988.

even when I turned away from it", which was "responsible for the government of the universe." He wrote that the experience had slightly weakened his conviction that death meant the end.

His confession of this may have embarrassed his supporters. In a later article he refined his view and wrote:

> What I should have said was that my experiences have weakened, not my belief that there is no life after death, but my inflexible attitude towards that belief ... my experiences have caused me to think that it was worth examining various possibilities of survival for their own sakes.

He described his previous attitude as "polemical" to the idea of an afterlife.[21]

Professor Ayer's new attitude meant that he changed sides on the issue about which William

Temple wrote so strongly, "The possibility, at least, of eternal life is indispensable to every

---

[21] *The Spectator*, 15th October 1988.

higher interest of man."[22]

The second convinced atheist was Anthony Flew. He was brought up in a Christian home; his father was a prominent Methodist. He became an atheist early in his life and wrote a famous attack on the arguments for God in his book *God and Philosophy*.[23] The book was influential. He never wavered in his atheism until his last years when, in 2010, he wrote a book[24] recording that he had become convinced by some of the arguments in favour of God's existence which he had spent his career rejecting. It seems that he held to his new found faith until his death, although some of his old admirers suggested that he had not been himself and had diminished powers when he became a believer. Whether that claim is relevant is far from evident. It is by no means

certain that technical brilliance at academic philosophy is needed to reach true conclusions

---

[22] See note 13, above.

[23] *God and Philosophy*, 1966.

[24] *There is a God*, 2010.

about God or the afterlife.

Professors Ayer and Flew are two further illustrations of the way in which experience of life and the use of reason work together to modify our attitude to God, often over long periods but sometimes urgently and suddenly.

9
Three Clues

THREE CLUES PROMPT ME to believe in another world beyond this material world, the realm of the eternal, everlasting life of the world to come.

John Stocks expressed one of the clues clearly and undogmatically, and all the more convincing for that. He asks us to accept it as true "at least for the sake of [his] argument", that our

> perception of temporal succession proves that [we] the perceiver is in some respect other than temporally successive, which is to say that the perceiver [each of us] has in some respect non-temporal or timeless being... [The] act of perception is the empirical guarantee of the perceiver's supra-temporal being.[25]

---

[25] *Time, Cause and Eternity*, p.143.

In his words, each of us is more, or other, than a "succession of conscious states" because, on the latter understanding of what a person is, a person or "self" would not be "capable of apprehending succession".[26]

To take a practical example, each of us is able to stand back from today's activities and events and *to think* about them in the light of what we have done or experienced earlier in our lives or of what we hope for in the future. Animals certainly learn and have memories; everyone with a dog or cat as a companion knows that, but we do not know, and have no reason to believe, that they can stand outside the present moment in the way we can. We know it for sure only of ourselves.

We may experience this in dramatic ways. For myself, when I think of Judy, my mind often turns to memories both of events in the days of 1965 when we first met and from the end of her life in May 2019, together with all sorts of happenings and activities together in

---

[26] Page 140.

between. I can "stand back" from all these memories; further, I can even stand back from the standing back, and soar above it all, learning lessons, many happy, a few sad, from our days on earth together. I can stand back from that act of standing back in that I can compare what I do with what God, in His being outside time, can do in relation to all human history and events. All of this is part of being a person, a being both temporal and non-temporal, in John Stock's words.

Philosophy has never satisfactorily explained what a "person" is. There is nothing other than God Himself, a Person but more than a Person, to compare it with, so there can be no illuminating analysis in terms of anything else. Our experience and thought, show that each person, each of us, is *more* than and other than a material object which is wholly determined by material cause and effect; more than an animal, however lovely, subject to stimulus and reaction. There is something timeless, non-temporal about us.

The second clue to our being more than and

other than material objects or animals, is in the realm of good and bad, right and wrong, and in our thinking about that realm.

Whenever we face a serious matter or action or event where questions of right and wrong, good and bad arise, we treat this as a real question. We try to work out which is which, and how that applies to the present case. This is particularly so when something affects us personally. People may *say* that they believe that right and wrong, good and bad are simply matters of convention, of different customs in different places. But if that person's own interests are involved, then it is another matter, a matter of finding out the truth – who is in the right and who is in the wrong. This applies particularly sharply when the interests at odds are those of greatly weaker and stronger parties. We just know that might is not, in itself, right.

We are more than material objects, more than animals. We have access to criteria and reasons that go beyond material cause and effect, beyond stimulus and response. This is especially clear in children, and from their early years. The charge that "this is not fair", as we often hear them say, is often true and goes very deep in human nature. This sense puts us in touch with the wonder-world, beyond this material world of cause and effect. It is a clue to the fact that the wonder-world is the realm of goodness.

The third clue lies in our being able to *think* and *reason* about such matters, and about mathematics, science, history and all manner of practical issues. What is going on when we do that? What is going on when we make a mistake, discover our mistake, stand back from it, and learn the lesson and correct it? Questions of true and false arise here, not just matters of convention or convenience, although it is convenient to discover the truth and avoid the falsehood.

When we do this sort of reasoning successfully, we believe that we reach the truth. We consciously move in our thinking step by step and so reach our conclusion. We, and our thoughts, are not simply a jumble of material cause and effects in a machine printing out what it does not grasp. It is preposterous to imagine that, without our conscious decisions and actions, all those thoughts and pieces of reasoning, as material events, would have taken place in a world without self-consciousness; and that Pythagoras' theorem would have been "proved" without a conscious and reasoning mind free to do so.

Our reasoning is conditioned by the arguments and the truth we seek, not determined by material cause and effect. That is what reasoning is. We have self-consciousness; we decide and take those steps. People may claim that the mechanistic explanation of cause and effect holds good for other people's reasoning, but always, and absurdly, they make an exception in their own favour, as if they alone had the ability to reason, while the rest of us were just machines. We know that they are wrong.

Our relation to time; the nature of good and bad, right and wrong; and our ability to reason, all point to our being more than and other than material objects or animals. They are clues pointing to a good wonder-world, beyond material cause and effect. It is in this wonder-world that there is the life of the world to come. [27]

---

[27] These questions interest me very much. I would like to write more, but this is not the place to do so. If you have become interested in them for the first time, I recommend *Mere Christianity* and *Miracles* by C.S. Lewis, and *The Freedom of the Will* by J.R. Lucas.

10

The Fourth Clue

THE FOURTH CLUE is Jesus of Nazareth. The first three clues were all matters of abstract thought and reason. How can a Person also be a *reason*? After all, Jesus lived for about thirty years, so long ago. No one doubts that, or that he died a horrible death. In fact, some people do deny that he really died on the Cross because it is too terrible for them to imagine, given what they believe about God, but all the evidence shows that their feelings get the better of their historical judgment.

But perhaps it is not so odd that a person should also be a reason for believing something. After all, our parents were people, and they were also the reasons, in part, why we believe what we do about family life. Judy, my wife, was (*is* for eternity, I believe) a person, and she is the reason why I believe so much of what I do about wives and husbands and married life.

But it is different with Jesus of Nazareth. He is the reason why I believe what I do about God, and I am not alone in this. My attitude has been shared with countless millions over the last twenty centuries.

How can this be?

This takes us back to part of what I said in my testimony to Judy at her funeral service, recorded in Chapter 3.

Within a very short time of Jesus' death and resurrection, his followers, who soon grew to be several thousand strong in and around Jerusalem, were speaking of him as a person, *but more than a person*. In the same way he had spoken of himself as "the Son of Man", a form of words so holy, because associated with Jesus' own words used of himself, that it is put into almost no one else's mouth in the New Testament.

For St Paul, Jesus was a person yet more

than a person immediately from the time of his conversion from devotion to Judaism (as it was understood by the Pharisees) to Jesus as Lord. In the account of his encounter with Jesus on the road to Damascus when he was converted, an account that can only be attributed plausibly to Paul himself, when Paul asks the Risen Jesus, "Who are you, Lord?", the reply is, "I am Jesus whom you are persecuting." For ever afterwards Paul saw Jesus as the Person, the corporate person or body, into whom Christian believers are incorporated. When he persecuted them, he was persecuting Jesus. He came to see Jesus as the One who constituted the purpose of all creation. All of this happened and was understood in this way within at most twenty years of Jesus' death and resurrection.

St Paul is not alone in his experience of Jesus Christ as a Being who is a person but more than an individual person in Whom we believers are incorporated. St Peter uses another metaphor, in his first letter. We believers are "living stones" built into a living house, a holy temple; and Jesus is himself the "living stone" which holds the whole building together. Jesus is the temple and through his grace, we are elements of it. Jesus says in the gospels, "If you destroy this temple [built by King Herod in Jerusalem], I will raise it again in three days [in the resurrection]."

Then again, take St John. He tells us how Jesus described himself to his closest disciples, on the night he was betrayed by one of them, as the vine, of which they were, and we now are, branches. Cut off from Him, we wither and die; united to Him, we live and bear fruit.

No one knows for sure the dates at which St John wrote his gospel or St Peter wrote his first letter. It is great good fortune that external events enable us to date several of St Paul's letters precisely. With St John and St Peter, good scholars have proposed a range of dates from the 60s AD for St Peter, to the end of the first century for St John, but some good scholars now believe that they both wrote before 70 AD when the Romans destroyed Jerusalem.

The point is this: the assessment and experience of Jesus as a person, but more than an individual human person, arose so quickly after Jesus' death and resurrection. And the resurrection of Jesus is surely the key. None of what followed would have happened without it.

Let us take the example of a great prophet, who was the founder of a great world religion, Mohammed. A good deal is known of him, of his struggles and victories (moral and military) of the devotion that he inspired in his followers, and of his death. Yet the important contrast with Jesus of Nazareth is that none of his devoted followers would claim that he is now alive and active as a person and more than an individual person. The Prophet was given by the Lord the Holy Koran to be the basis of a new society. Muslims have a great reverence for the Prophet, praying the words "Blessed be he" after a mention of his name. There is a clue in that. Mohammed is a man; it is for us to pray that he be blessed by the Lord.

For a Muslim to equate the Prophet with God is a blasphemy. For Christians, to equate Jesus Christ with God the Father, united with the Holy Spirit, ever One God, is the essence of their faith. St Paul wrote of the destiny of each of us to appear, in the life of the world to come, before the judgment seat of God in one place[28] and in another before the judgment seat of Christ[29] There was no distinction in his mind. For a devout Muslim, the idea that we should appear before Mohammed for judgment in Paradise would be a blasphemy.

Without doubt, it all goes back to how Jesus perceived Himself and was perceived by those around Him in his life, as a person but more than an individual person, and to His resurrection which made sense of it all.

What can anyone say of Christ's resurrection? Certainly, nothing new; so much has it been discussed and spoken of and written about, as well as experienced by Christians, to this day.

Everyone knows that it is all but impossible to make one step by step account of the events and actions on the day of Jesus' resurrection

---

[28] Letter to the Romans, chapter 14, verse 10.
[29] Second Letter to the Corinthians, chapter 5, verse 10.

and the days which followed it. The records take us from the discovery early on Sunday morning that the tomb was empty, through the many resurrection appearances on that and the following days recorded in the gospels and in St Paul's first letter to the Corinthians, chapter fifteen, to his Ascension into heaven forty days later.

The stories are like the strands of a cobweb, shooting off in different directions, yet somehow the web is made of steel. It defies destruction.

Perhaps the best representation of it was not written by an academic, but by Dorothy L. Sayers in the final play in her series of twelve dramas on the life of Christ, *The Man Born to be King*, dating from the Second World War. Miss Sayers (who was also the creator of Lord Peter Wimsey) writes her plays, particularly this last one about the Resurrection, with the eye of a scholar and poet. Her powerful argument, explicit in her dialogue, is that if Jesus did not rise but his body was still lying, dead, in the tomb, it was overwhelmingly in the interests of the religious authorities, the Jewish

Sanhedrin, and of the Roman power, Pontius Pilate, to search out and display the body. They did not do so because they could not. The asperity of the words that Miss Sayers puts in the mouth of Caiaphas the High Priest does full justice to the impossible position of those in power. How could they deny the truth? What line, what policy could they possibly follow? One of Caiaphas' colleagues in the Sanhedrin is imagined as putting this question to him.

> *Shadrach*: And what is our policy, Most Venerable?
>
> *Caiaphas*: Can you ask? ... Naturally, we shall deny the story... The weakness of our position, of course, is that we cannot produce the body.
>
> *1st Elder*: We shall leave no stone unturned!
>
> *Caiaphas*: Certainly. But in case it should prove undiscoverable –
>
> *2nd Elder*: Undiscoverable! It must be somewhere.
>
> *Caiaphas*: I said, in case.
>
> *3rd Elder*: Can't we just re-seal the tomb and pretend that nothing has happened?

Caiaphas: In a public garden? In broad day-light? ... And suppose Pilate should hear rumours and order the tomb to be examined

2nd Elder (brilliantly): Why not substitute another corpse?

Caiaphas: Having first crucified it, I suppose, by way of lending verisimilitude... It would be simpler to stick to the truth.

Shadrach: The truth being –?

Caiaphas: Really, Brother Shadrach! ... The body was stolen, of course... Unless anybody agrees with poor, afflicted Nicodemus ... No? ... Then we must deal at once with these Levites .... Clerk, ask Captain Elihu to step this way ... Incidentally, gentlemen, pray note that this discussion has not taken place. No record of it will appear in the minutes. There will be a trifling disbursement from the Temple funds to be accounted for. It had better, perhaps, be debited to – er – educational purposes ...

Without the resurrection of Jesus, there would have been an end to the matter, yet another failed splinter group in Judaism; yet another brief disorder, horribly put down by the governor, Pontius Pilate, and Roman soldiers.

But it was *not* the end to the matter. Christ rose. Solely on the basis of that, Christian faith was born and the New Testament was written. Their existence would be an inexplicable riddle without the resurrection; a phenomenon with no cause. Jesus, without his resurrection would simply have disappeared. But Jesus rose and the assurance of the life of the world to come was given to the faithful, and in St Paul we read the undoubted truth "If for this life only we have hope in Christ, we are, of all people, the most to be pitied."[30]

If we are not to be pitied it is solely because the hope is true.

---

[30] First letter to the Corinthians, chapter 15.

11

The Final Enemy
and the Final Clue

YESTERDAY AFTERNOON, as the sun began to set, I was looking at the glorious flower bed that Judy designed in the last months of her life. There are flowers of all sorts, all colours, all heights, all shapes and textures. It is a wonder. She discussed it with me, arranged for the bed, till then composed of intractable clay, to be filled with good top soil, and left me with a list of plants and a map for the planting. The bed is a glory.

Strangely, it gives me a feeling of what it would be like without a faith in and a knowledge of the life of the world to come. The flowers in this bed will fade, wither and die.

Come the autumn and winter rains, and perhaps snow, the bed will be bedraggled, sometimes with standing puddles of rain in it. If left to itself, it will flower again next year, and the year after, but gradually it will become less lovely, with less of Judy in it. It is akin to living on "in people's memories", as they say. The people with the memories, in turn, die and they are lost. That is the way of the world. We all know that.

But Jesus says, "I have overcome the world," and His followers share that victory. Although part of Judy's bequest to this world is in that flower bed, Judy herself is alive in the spirit, in the Lord, and is still active.

Jesus overcame death. St Paul writes that "Death is swallowed up in victory," the victory of the Risen Christ. He called death "the final enemy", defeated by Christ (his first letter to the Corinthians, chapter 15).

The final clue is different from the others. This clue is entirely within you. No one but you has direct access to it. It is what is happening in your heart and mind, the two of them working together, as we have seen throughout this book.

It is worth asking yourself, what has been going on within your heart and mind as you have been thinking about these questions?

Heart and mind. A good example for me, at least, of their relation goes back to the days not long after Judy was diagnosed with cancer. The shock for her hardly bears thinking about, and it was also a great shock for me. How could the two of us, and each of us, keep going?

At that time Judy gave me a note on a yellow "Post-it". I still have it beside our bed: "You will have courage because you will have hope," words from the Book of Job, chapter 11, verse 18. And a little later in the book we read of the substance of the hope, "I know that my Redeemer lives... And after my skin has been destroyed, yet in my flesh I will see God; I myself will see Him with my own eyes", chapter 19, verses 26-7.

It was a great profession of faith by the unknown writer of the Book of Job, uttered so many years before Jesus' coming. We have a great advantage; I almost feel that it is unfair. We know of Jesus' resurrection and of his direct promise to us that we shall be with Him in the life of the world to come (Gospel of St John, chapter 14.)

They go together, heart and mind; fact and hope. God means us to use and follow both, held closely together.

If we rely on hope and heart alone, we may find ourselves lurching between ecstasy and despair. We might (God forbid) find ourselves dabbling in spiritualism, associating with those who claim to summon up the spirits of the dead. Perhaps they really succeed in doing it. Whether or not that is so, it is a tragic and mistaken path. Read the story of King Saul's visit to the Witch of Endor for that purpose in the First Book of Samuel, chapter 28, in the Old Testament, and Kipling's great poem on that incident, "En-dor", and you will wish, under God, to protect yourself from taking that path.

Oh, the road to En-dor is the oldest road,
And the craziest road of all!

Straight it runs to the Witch's abode
As it did in the days of Saul,
And nothing has changed of the sorrow in
*   store*
For such as go down on the road to En-dor.

It is through Jesus alone that we come into God's presence. Jesus is the only mediator, or *medium,* if you will, between us and God.

The danger of following mind and fact too much is that we never grasp the significance of it all; we devote all our time to fascinating philosophical or historical or theological questions and debates. For my part, I love such matters and cannot get enough of them. But, taking heart and mind together, I know that I must let myself see the wood as a whole as well as the individual trees.

The *wood* is the overwhelming truth of the Risen Christ and His promise to us of life with Him in the world to come.

In some famous words,

There are ... only three things we can do about death: to desire it, to fear it, or to ignore it. The third alternative, which is the one the modern world calls "healthy", is surely the most uneasy and precarious of all.[31]

It is never too late for Jesus to take us to Himself. Everything depends on Jesus.

"Lord, put into my heart a longing for my heavenly home."

---

[31] C.S. Lewis in a letter dated 7th June 1959 addressed to Mary Willis Shelbourne (*Collected Letters*, Vol. III page 1056)